AF471231

A Source Book of Passenger Vehicles

Early Paris horse-bus.

A Source Book of
Passenger Vehicles

Compiled by the Olyslager Organisation
Edited by Bart H. Vanderveen

WARD LOCK LIMITED · LONDON

ISBN 0 7063 1468 9

First published in Great Britain 1973
by Ward Lock Limited, 116 Baker Street,
London, W1M 2BB

Designed by Conal Buck

Text filmset in 7 pt Univers (689)
and printed and bound in England by
Cox and Wyman Ltd,
London, Fakenham and Reading

Foreword

The term 'passenger vehicles' encompasses a variety of motor vehicles but mainly buses, coaches and personnel carriers, all intended to carry more passengers than can be accommodated in a conventional private car.

In this Source Book we have set out to portray examples of most if not all these different types and at the same time to present an historical survey in the same way as in our other Source Books, namely those dealing with Commercial and Military Vehicles. Those readers who are not too familiar with the subject will, when leafing through this book, realize how complex and diversified the passenger vehicle industry has become and they will not be surprised to learn that a lot of people have made it their whole-hearted hobby in a variety of ways. There are those who ardently collect fleet numbers, time-tables, pictures and other items appertaining to specific operators and others who go all the way and acquire a derelict bus or coach for rebuilding and preservation. This is particularly so in Great Britain, where in events like the Historic Commercial Vehicle Club's annual London-to-Brighton Run, countless examples of painstakingly restored vehicles can be admired. Catering for these and other enthusiasts there are clubs such as the PSV Circle and The Omnibus Society, in addition to the HCVC already mentioned.

It has been stated that there are two types of buses: London buses and 'all the others'. Whether one agrees with this or not, it must be said that the 'London bus' is indeed a story in itself and one which forms an important part of the history of British bus makers, particularly AEC. Thanks are extended to the manufacturers and individuals who assisted us with photographs and to Mr David Hurley for valuable editorial comments.

Piet Olyslager M S I A, M S A E, K I V I

Introduction

The development of the 'mechanized' omnibus may be traced back to the sixteenth century when Berthold Holzschuher, who tried to find a way of transporting a group of people without the use of horses, constructed a muscle-powered vehicle. It ran in 1560 in Nuremberg, powered by eight crank-operating men and carrying another eight. 'Benetto' was the name given to this contraption by its inventor.

Then about 1600 there was the famous Dutch Sail-Carriage of Simon Stevin, virtually a ship on wheels with the rear axle steering and capable of 34 kmh/21 mph while carrying some 30 passengers. It ran on the beaches between Petten and Scheveningen and was in use for six years. It would appear that the French mathematician and philosopher Blaise Pascal (1623–62) was the first to introduce horse-buses in Paris. These were, at first, intended primarily for the transport of infirm people and the sick.

In the nineteenth century, several steam-propelled coaches appeared in Britain: those of Gurney and James about 1828–9, Church in 1823–33, etc. The latter built a 50-seater for use on the London–Birmingham route. Not long afterwards the Frenchman, Etienne Lenoir (1822–1900), obtained a patent for his gas engine but it was to be some time before a serious competitor for the horse appeared on the road. Meanwhile the horse-bus became an established part of city traffic in Paris and London. The Paris enterprise by 1880 had some 800 horse-buses in service and a few years later was reorganized into the *Compagnie Générale des Omnibus.* In London there was the London General Omnibus Company, which in 1880 owned about 600 of the 810 horse-buses then operating on London's streets.

The first motorbus dates from 1895, when Carl Benz built an eight-seater on an 1894-type car chassis. Gottlieb Daimler produced his first bus in 1899, after a Daimler goods chassis had been fitted with a bus body for a London customer in the previous year. From then on progress was rapid. Many truck chassis were fitted with single-

GM Intercity Coach of the 1960s.

or double-decker bodywork and other chassis were designed and produced specifically for this purpose, the famous London 'B'-Type being a classic example.

It is probably true to say that until after World War II the majority of the world's buses were built on truck chassis or derivations of them. Today the picture is totally different and most buses are specially designed for their purpose, the main exception being the typical American 'school-bus' which in most cases is a utility-type all-metal body on a long-wheelbase commercial chassis supplied at relatively low cost by one of the American 'Big Three': General Motors (Chevrolet, GMC), Ford and Chrysler (Dodge).

In addition to the motorbus, which was a direct development from the horse-drawn bus, there is another important type of passenger-carrying vehicle, namely the motor coach. This type is of a more (often much more) luxurious nature, being intended for longer-distance travel as compared with the bus which is used strictly for relatively short hauls with a larger number of passengers. The coach was originally developed from the horse-drawn charabanc, an open vehicle with transverse bench seats (hence the original French word *Char-à-bancs* (literally: carriage with benches). Consequently the first self-propelled charabancs were large open touring cars with five or more rows of seats. Typically they were used to carry groups of people to seaside resorts and the like. By the late 1920s, the charabancs had developed into luxurious carriages with full weather protection (All-Weather Coaches) and it was not long before coaches were almost exclusively of the fully-enclosed type, often with large observation windows and usually with a folding roof. The development of both the bus and the coach was influenced to a large extent by legislation in the country of use. Such legislation was and is a very involved subject and has at times had a retarding effect on bus design.

For some time the horse- and motor-bus shared in public transport.

AEC double-decker of New York's Fifth Avenue Coach Company.

Czechoslovakian Tatra T86 trolleybus of 1938.

On the other hand it protected the bonafide PSV (Public Service Vehicle) operators from the practices of the so-called 'pirates' of earlier days. Following this introduction is a summary of public service vehicles regulations as applicable in Great Britain forty years ago.

Finally there is the category of personnel carriers. These are vehicles intended for the carrying of office and factory personnel to and from work, inter-factory transport, etc. Sometimes they are buses or coaches which have completed a useful service life but are still fit for several more years of use. Nowadays we see many small buses ('mini-buses') being used for this purpose. These are modifications of modern 'box-type' panel vans as produced by most of the major vehicle manufacturers. Of course there have been many variations in the above categories. There have been trailer, semi-trailer and articulated buses, electrically-propelled (trolley) buses, one-and-a-half and double-deck coaches, 100-seater semi-trailer personnel carriers, all-wheel-drive military troop-carriers, half-track buses, and many more.

Public Service Vehicles (PSVs)
Following is a summary of PSV regulations as applying in Great Britain at the beginning of the 1930s:

For the purpose of the control and licensing of PSVs — e.g. omnibuses and charabancs — Great Britain is divided into 13 traffic areas, 11 in England and two in Scotland. In each of these areas there are three commissioners (except in London, where there is only one), and these are

South African Thornycroft SA/GRN6/1 cross-country bus.

German Kässbohrer trolleybus with trailer in 1939.

responsible for the issue, suspension and revocation of all licences required by PSVs. They are appointed by the Minister of Transport.

Outside London one of the three commissioners is selected by the Minister from a panel nominated by the County Councils of the area, another from a panel nominated by the councils of the county boroughs and urban districts, and the third is such a person as the Minister may think fit to appoint as chairman. The chairman holds office for not more than seven years and the other commissioners for not more than three years.

Public service vehicles are of three kinds:

(1) Stage carriages — that is, vehicles such as omnibuses, which carry passengers at separate fares (any or all of which are less than 1s.), stage by stage, stopping to pick up and set down passengers along the line of route;

(2) Express carriages — that is, vehicles such as charabancs, which carry passengers to

Britain's first 30-ft long PSV after the 1930 C & U Act: a Northern General Short-bodied 44-seater six-wheeler (6×2), converted to four-wheeler in 1941.

one or more common destinations at separate fares (none of which is less than 1s.). The requirement that all fares must be over 1s. is intended to prevent express carriages competing unfairly with stage carriages by carrying passengers for short journeys;

(3) Contract carriages; vehicles hired for reward under one contract for the use of the vehicle as a whole — e.g. a coach hired to take a football team to a match. Vehicles which are normally used in agriculture, trade or business are considered to be contract carriages, if on any occasion they are used, even without reward, to carry eight or more passengers, unless the passengers are work-people carried in the course of their employment.

No one may use or allow any other person to use a vehicle as a PSV unless he holds the appropriate licence for it. A vehicle may be licensed either as a stage, express or contract carriage. A vehicle licensed as a stage carriage may be used as an express carriage or contract carriage, and one licensed as an express carriage may be used as a contract carriage with the consent of the local traffic commissioners.

Local authorities may make orders determining the roads which may be used by public service vehicles (in London, for example, the central area is closed to certain types of PSVs), and may set up stopping places at which vehicles may stop for a longer time than is necessary for the taking up and setting down of passengers.

Road Service Licences. Before anyone can run a service of stage carriages or express carriages on any route the service must be approved by the commissioners and a road service licence obtained.

Prototype design of new transit bus concept, to be developed under Urban Mass Transportation Administration programme by American Motors.

Early Leyland 'chara', complete with roof and side curtains.

Attractive Thornycroft 'observation coach' of the 1930s, operated in Brazil.

The PSV licence relates to the vehicle, the road service licence to the route on which it is to operate.

Every person applying for a road service licence must submit particulars of his vehicles and (if it is a regular service) of the time-tables and fare-tables, and maximum and minimum fares may be fixed by the commissioners. It may be made a condition of the licence that these fares are charged.

A road service licence is only valid in the traffic area for which it is granted, and licences for services running through several areas must be 'backed' by the commissioners of each area. A road service licence may be revoked if any of the conditions on which it is granted are broken frequently or wilfully, or after one innocent breach if danger is caused to the public.

Drivers' and Conductors' Licences. Special licences must be obtained for drivers and conductors of PSVs. Every driver must be over 21 and every conductor over 18, except where the

Citroën-Kégresse *Autochenille*
for use in North Africa.

person applying was regularly employed as a driver or conductor of a PSV in the last six months of 1929. These licences may be revoked or suspended by the commissioners by whom they were granted on account of the conduct or physical disability of the holder.

The applicant for a driver's or conductor's licence must provide evidence of his ability to read and write, a reference from a previous employer and a certificate as to character. He must also undergo a medical examination, and the applicant for a driver's licence must pass a driving test. When the licence is granted, a badge is issued which must be worn while the holder is on duty. Regulations have also been made as to the conduct of drivers and conductors.

Public service vehicle licences are obtained from the traffic commissioners of the area in which the vehicle is intended to be ordinarily operated, road service licences from the commissioners of any traffic area entered by the route, and drivers' and conductors' licences from the commissioners of the area in which the applicant resides. All these licences, except road service licences, remain in

**Streamlining gone berserk: 'Trambus' on
Büssing-NAG 350T chassis, 1935–7.**

force for a year from the date on which they are granted unless revoked before that time. Road service licences expire on certain prescribed dates in the yesar. All these licences are in addition to the ordinary driving licence and road tax licences.

Passengers must also conform to certain regulations as to their conduct while on the vehicle. A fire extinguisher and first-aid apparatus must be carried.

Persons employed by the holder of a road service licence are entitled to the same wages and conditions of employment as those fixed by a resolution of the House of Commons for persons employed in carrying out a contract with a Government department.

For the protection of passengers in PSVs, it is provided that any clause in the contract of carriage which in any way negatives or restricts the liability of the owner of the vehicle or of any other person in respect of the death or bodily injury of any passenger while being carried in, entering or alighting from the vehicle, shall be void.

These regulations are still substantially the same today.

Old buses in captivity. Left: 1949 Albion CX19
(used for Australia–UK–Australia trips),
right: 1948 AEC RT3, one of London Transport's
famous 'RT'-Types.

Bus chassis are used also for bodies like
pantechnicons and mobile showrooms:
Commer 'Avenger' of Scottish Gas Board, 1957.

Native bus taking shape on a MAN 415H truck
chassis in Nigeria, early 1960s.

1898 Daimler (D)
10 PS

Having started life as a private car (Daimler-*Viktoriawagen*), this vehicle was rebodied and modified to be used as a passenger vehicle. It had seating accommodation for 10 passengers in the main body, which was all-enclosed, and was operated on the route Künzelsau–Bad Mergentheim in 1898. The operator was the firm of Motorwagenbetrieb Kunzelsau–Mergentheim GmbH. The bus had tiller steering and full-elliptic front springs. Final drive was by chains.

1905 Büssing (D)
Double-decker

Among the earliest London buses were many Büssings, supplied through Straker & Squire, Engineers, of 9, Bushlane, London EC, who later built them under licence. They were operated by the London General Omnibus Co. Ltd (shown), the London Road Car Co. Ltd, etc. and during 1904–6 some 400 Büssing double-deckers were taken into service. Noteworthy were the low position of the radiator, just visible between the front wheels, and the towing attachment, visible to the right of the rear mud wing, two early Büssing characteristics.

1905 Thornycroft (GB)
30 HP

Following their early efforts to popularize the steam-driven bus, examples of which were used in Burma (1900) and London (1902), Thornycroft of Basingstoke developed passenger vehicles based on their contemporary 2- and 2½-ton goods chassis in 1904. They had four-cylinder petrol engines which for an additional charge of £25 could be made to run on kerosene fuel. When the London and South Western Railway Company took delivery of a 'Thorny' to inaugurate a bus service between Farnham and Haslemere in Surrey in 1905, the vehicle was driven by a fitter from the Basingstoke factory and, in order to observe the passengers' reaction to the new venture, the Company's sales manager acted as conductor.

1906 Albion (GB)
16 HP A3

The Albion A3 chassis was in production
by Albion Motors Ltd in Scotstoun near
Glasgow, Scotland, during the period
1904 to 1915. The 12-seater charabanc
illustrated here was delivered to Irish
Motor Services in 1906. The vehicle had
a four-cylinder side-valve petrol engine,
rated at 16 hp, transmission final drive by
chain and solid rubber tyres on wooden
wheels (dual tyres on single wheels at
rear). It was used on the Kingstown to
Bray route, near Dublin.

1907 FIAT (I)
18–24 HP

The FIAT 18–24 hp Omnibus chassis was produced during the four years 1906–10 and had a 3.40-metre wheelbase and 1500-kg carrying capacity. The weight of the complete chassis was 1450 kg. The four-cylinder $4\frac{1}{2}$-litre engine developed 24 hp at 1400 rpm and had low-tension magneto ignition. It drove the separate four-speed gearbox via a multi-disc clutch. The gearbox incorporated the jackshaft/differential, which drove the rear wheels by chains. The foot brake acted on the transmission, the hand brake on the rear wheels.

1908 Daimler (D)
35 PS

The German Daimler Motoren Gesellschaft had factories at Bad Cannstatt near Stuttgart and at Marienfelde near Berlin. This vehicle was produced in the latter works and such vehicles were therefore also known as Marienfeldes (products from the Cannstatt works were often referred to as Cannstatt-Daimlers). The bus shown was based on a 3-ton truck chassis and was supplied about 1908 to the Bayerischen Post (Bavarian postal authority). Its 35 hp four-cylinder engine drove the heavy back axle via a shaft.

S. A. R.

1909 Dennis (GB) 30 HP

Before World War I, the South African Railways ordered several vehicles from Dennis Bros Ltd in Guildford, Surrey, and amongst them was this station bus, produced about 1909. It provided seated accommodation for 18 passengers, all facing forward, in the main body which had its entrance in the front wall in the form of a sliding door next to the driver's seat. Note the mailbox fitted next to this door and the large single headlight.

1910–20 AEC/LGOC (GB)
'B'-Type

After building 61 experimental 'X'-Type chassis for double-deck omnibuses in 1909, the Company, which was incorporated as the Associated Equipment Company (AEC) in 1912, went on to produce over 3000 units of the immortal 'B'-Type. Powered by a 30 hp four-cylinder petrol engine, this 34-seater open-top double-decker was built on a flitch-plated ash frame and featured a cone clutch, three-speed silent chain gearbox, worm-driven back axle and worm and nut steering. About 3000 were in operation in London by August 1914 when war broke out, and many of these were commandeered by the War Department for use as troop carriers. The bus shown is 'Ole Bill' a survivor, carrying some of the veterans who rode on them in France in 1914–15. The bus is now on display in the Imperial War Museum in London.

1911 Saurer (CH)
30 PS

Based on a Swiss Saurer shaft-drive truck chassis was the first German Kässbohrer *Linien-Omnibus*. It featured wooden wheels (twin rear) with solid rubber tyres and paraffin lamps. The maximum speed was about 30 mph. The bodywork offered accommodation for 18 seated passengers and 10 standing and the complete vehicle cost 18,000 Marks. It was operated on the Wiblingen–Ulm route and is shown here with the founder of the well-known Kässbohrer concern, Karl Kässbohrer (1864–1922) on the left.

1912 Daimler (GB)
Double-decker

The British Daimler Motor Co. Ltd of
Coventry had been formed in 1898 and
produced motor vehicles of various kinds
including commercial types. In 1912 the
London MET (Metropolitan Electric Tramways) placed a large order for double-
decker buses, which were subsequently
operated by the LGOC (London General
Omnibus Co.). By the time World War I
broke out, some 240 of the 350 Daimlers
ordered had been delivered and these
were all commandeered by the Government for use by the Army and Admiralty
both at home and in France. They had
'Silent Knight' sleeve-valve four-cylinder
engines. The body shown was not the
original. Many Daimlers were supplied
in chassis form to the Government and
fitted with standard military GS (general
service) bodywork. In many respects
these Daimlers resembled the AEC/LGOC
'B'-Type chassis.

1913 Commer (GB)
WP 3

This 16-seater 'shooting brake', affection-ately known as 'Yellow Peril', was owned by Rootes Ltd, to whom Commer Cars Ltd belonged, for many years. It was splendidly restored, probably to better than original condition and appeared in many rallies and similar events. It had a 25 hp four-cylinder engine which drove through a leather-lined cone clutch and a three-speed preselective transmission. Final drive, from jackshaft to rear wheels, was by enclosed chains. Picture shows HRH Princess Margaret touring the Royal Show at Stoneleigh Abbey, Warwickshire. The vehicle's first owner was Lord Lonsdale.

1914 Dennis (GB)
40 HP

Dennis Brothers in Guildford supplied
buses to many operators and it would
appear that a large portion of the vehicles
were delivered complete, i.e. with Dennis-
built bodywork, especially charabancs.
This single-decker Public Service bus
was supplied to Chesterfield Corporation
Tramways and afforded accommodation
for 25 passengers inside and 3 outside.
The centre-hinged folding ladder at the
back led to the roof where goods could
be carried. The engine was a four-cylinder
40 hp unit and the rear axle was of the
worm-drive type.

31

1915 FIAT (I)
18 BC

The 18 BC bus chassis was derived from the contemporary FIAT 18 BL truck of which large numbers saw military service in World War I. It weighed 2400 kg and was produced until 1919. In the complete form shown here it had accommodation for 14 to 18 passengers. The four-cylinder engine had a capacity of 4578 cc and developed 25 bhp at 1200 rpm. Transmission comprised a multi-disc clutch, four-speed gearbox and enclosed chain final drive. Wheelbase was 3.25 metres, overall length 4.85 metres. The solid rubber tyres measured 900×100 at front, 1050×140 at rear. Maximum speed was 17 mph.

1919 Daimler (D)
Post-Omnibus

This smart little bus, produced by the Daimler Motoren Gesellschaft just after World War I, was operated by the postal authorities of Württemberg, a state in Southern Germany of which Stuttgart was the capital. Daimler had been producing motor vehicles at near-by Cannstatt since 1896 and, in 1925–6, merged with Benz to form Daimler-Benz. The product name, however, became Mercedes-Benz. The bus shown featured shaft-drive to the rear axle and solid rubber tyres, dual at rear.

1919 Magirus (D)
2CV110 Post-Omnibus

The first Magirus Omnibus was manufactured and delivered in the autumn of 1919. It was put into service by the Württembergische Post. The 18-seater bodywork, made of wood and panelled with sheet metal, was mounted on a 3-ton Magirus truck chassis of conventional layout with four-cylinder water-cooled 40 bhp engine. It had a foot brake which operated on a drum behind the four-speed gearbox and which could be cooled with water from a reservoir by the driver's side during long descents. It featured shaft-drive, solid tyres (dual rear) and a sprag (hill holder). The wheelbase was 3.91 metres, the overall length 5.90 metres and the height 3.10 metres.

1920 Crossley (GB)
25/30 HP

During World War I, Crossley Motors Ltd of Gorton, Manchester, produced many thousands of vehicles for the Royal Flying Corps (RFC, later RAF) and after the war production was continued with very little change. Post-war as well as reconditioned wartime chassis were frequently used as a basis for 14-seater buses. This one was one of a small fleet run by the Middlesex operators Filkins & Ainsworth, shown after takeover by the London Passenger Transport Board. Note the dual rear tyres, a feature of many Crossleys of the period.

1920-1 AEC (GB)
'K'-Type

The 'K'-Type bus was announced by the LGOC in August 1919 and 1157 of them were produced during the following two years. This model introduced forward control with the driver situated beside the engine, which enabled the carrying capacity to be increased to 46 passengers, it had transverse seats. The power unit was rated at 28 hp and was of the four-cylinder petrol type. The engine auxiliaries were mounted on the left-hand side because as a result of the forward driver's position the opposite side was rather inaccessible for routine maintenance work. The vehicle shown was in service with the East Surrey Traction Co. Ltd, whose badge it carried on the radiator.

1921 Büssing (D)
Doppelstock-Omnibus

Heinrich Büssing was one of Germany's pioneers in bus manufacture and as early as 1904, Büssing supplied buses to the London General Omnibus Company. Altogether the LGOC received 328 double-decker buses from Büssing and their British licencee, Straker-Squire. Illustrated here is a 42-seater *Doppelstock* (double-decker) model produced in 1921 for the *Allgemeiner Berliner Omnibus Aktiengesellschaft* or Berlin General Omnibus Company. It featured an open-top open-sided upper deck with open staircase and right-hand drive.

1922 AEC (GB)
'S'-Type

The AEC 'S'-Type was larger and more powerful than its predecessor, the 'K'-Type. It was a 54-seater open-top double-decker and during the years 1921 to 1923 a total of 1066 were produced in several versions (Models 401, 402, 403, 404). The 403 for example, was the provincial version, appearing in 1922. Although it bore a strong resemblance to the earlier 'K'-Type its weight exceeded the then permitted legal maximum of 7 tons. The vehicle, subjected to exhaustive tests, finally convinced the authorities that a heavier bus was safe and as a result the maximum legal laden weight was raised to $8\frac{1}{2}$ tons. A 403 in the livery of the East Surrey Traction Co. Ltd, whose headquarters were in Reigate, is shown.

1923 Chevrolet (USA)
Series D

The Chevrolet 'Utility Express' Series D 120-inch wheelbase chassis was rated at 1 ton and sold at $550. It was frequently used as the basis for a bus or coach, often of the *Char-à-Bancs* type. The four-cylinder overhead-valve engine, clutch and transmission were the same as used in the contemporary Chevrolet 'Superior' Series B passenger car. The front springs were of the quarter-elliptic type; hence the chassis frame did not have the usual 'dumb irons'. Front tyres were 31×4, rear tyres single 34×4½. The bus shown was operated in Ginneken, Netherlands.

1923 Dennis (GB)
40 HP

This attractive silver-painted 29-seater charabanc belonged to
the Northern Ireland operators Mourne Mountains Touring
Company Ltd in Rostrevor. It was based on a conventional
shaft-drive solid-tyred truck chassis with four-cylinder 40 hp
engine. Note the many side doors, the folded top and the full-
length running boards.

1924 Büssing (D)
VI GL Dreiachser

Büssing was the world's first large-scale producer of six-wheeled
passenger vehicles and trucks. Heavy six-wheeled Büssings
with large pneumatic tyres first appeared in 1923. It was claimed
that during the 1920s Büssing supplied 98% of all the six-
wheelers in Germany and about 50% of those abroad. One of
a fleet of three-axle Büssing buses is shown that were operated
by the Hamburger Hochbahn AG (HHA). Note the large tyres,
size 42×9 (1150×250). The engine was a water-cooled
overhead-valve six-cylinder petrol unit and the mechanical
brakes worked on the four rear wheels. It was in production
until 1927.

HHA
CONTINENTAL CORD

1924 Reo (USA)
'Speed Wagon'

Now a regular entry in historic vehicles rallies, this was one of many English-bodied Reo 'Speed Wagons' operated in Britain during the 1920s when home-built vehicles tended to be heavy and underpowered. Basically this was a RHD 25-cwt truck chassis with $34 \times 4\frac{1}{2}$ inch pneumatic tyres on detachable-rim wood or steel wheels, single at the rear. The engine was a $4\frac{1}{8} \times 4\frac{1}{2}$ inch four-cylinder, rated at 27.2 hp, which drove through a multi-plate clutch, three-speed gearbox and spiral-bevel final drive with 4.7:1 gear ratio. The wheelbase was 10 ft 8 in, the track 4 ft 8 in. The chassis weighed $23\frac{1}{2}$ cwt and sold at £295. This one was preserved by Mr J. Hirst of Halifax, Yorkshire.

1925 Dennis (GB)
'E'-Series

Birch Bros Ltd, of which Mr William H. Birch was managing director, were among the relatively few operators in the London area to take delivery of buses on Dennis Bros' 'E'-Series (or EV) chassis which had been introduced at the 1925 Olympia Show. The Birch-operated specimen shown was a standard-sized single-decker with rear entrance. It had forward-control on the right-hand side and no windscreen for the driver, as was usual at that time. The driver was provided with a storm apron, which was suspended at chin-height.

1926 SD (GB)
'Freighter'

Based on the well-known SD 'Freighter' chassis this windowless 'Tramocar' bus was used along the waterfront of Worthing, Sussex. Produced by Shelvoke & Drewry Ltd of Letchworth, Hertfordshire, it featured extremely small, solid rubber-shod wheels and a transversally-mounted four-cylinder petrol engine under the driver's seat. Driving controls were tram-style twin tillers, one on either side of the centrally-seated driver. The one on the right controlled the three-speed epicyclic gearbox, on the opposite was the handle for tiller steering. One could drive the vehicle standing and facing either direction. The chassis were used by many municipal cleansing organizations, mainly as dustcarts. The standard fare board on this bus reads: 'West to East 2d'.

1927 ADC (GB)
419

ADC was the trademark of Associated Daimler Co. Ltd, a short-lived amalgamation of AEC and Daimler marketing interests (1926–9). AEC was originally situated in Blackhorse Lane, Walthamstow, East London, but moved to Southall in 1927. In that year, the LGOC purchased some 115 single-deckers, including about 30 All-Weather coaches with roll-back canvas top and half forward-control layout, all of which went to the East Surrey Traction Co. fleet, based at Reigate, Surrey. The total number of Model 419 chassis produced was listed by AEC as 39, all in 1927. During the period of sales-cooperation, AECs were sold under their own name in London, but as ADCs elsewhere.

1927 ADC (GB)
'NS'-Type

The 'NS'-Type bus was introduced by AEC in 1923 and was the first double-decker with a drop-frame. Originally they were supplied with solid tyres on cast-spoke wheels. Final deliveries, during 1926–7, carried the ADC (Associated Daimler) radiator although the same AEC engine was used. Many were later fitted with driver's windscreens. The one shown was operated from Reigate by the East Surrey Traction Company. The 'NS' had a low centre of gravity, achieved by pressed steel chassis side members cranked behind the front axle and over the double-reduction rear axle, also allowing for a single-step platform and a possible roof for the upper deck. Authority decreed, however, that the roof could not be fitted and licences were not granted for the fully-enclosed type to operate until two years later.

1927 Chevrolet (USA)
Series LM

The Chevrolet 'Utility Express' model for the year 1927 was designated Series LM and was also called 'Capitol'. It had much in common with the contemporary Chevrolet passenger car but a four-speed gearbox was optional and frame, springs and axles were built for a higher payload. Cheap and reliable, the four-cylinder Chevrolet chassis was used for many types of bodywork, including bus and coach. This little bus, which looks rather 'over-bodied', was in service with Magnet, a small operator in Surrey. Front wheel brakes did not appear on Chevrolets until the Series LP, late in the following year.

1928 Gilford (GB)
166SD

During the late 1920s and throughout the 1930s, Gilford buses and coaches were used by many British operators. They were known for their American six-cylinder engines (Buda, Lycoming) and low-swept chassis frames. From December 1927 the company was located in High Wycombe, Bucks, but after 1935 no more vehicles were produced. The Gilford Motor Co. still exists, however, at Ixworth, Suffolk, owned by Mr Prince Marshall. The bus shown was acquired by the London Passenger Transport Board in about 1933 and was one of thirteen originally delivered to Skylark Motor Coaches of London W1.

1928 Leyland (GB)
'Lioness' LTB1

This impressive-looking 'bonneted' (normal-control) Leyland 'Lioness' was first registered in Flintshire, North Wales, in late 1928 and was supplied new to Brooke Bros of Rhyl. The body, by Burlingham, was of the All-Weather type, which differed from the earlier charabancs in having one entrance and full weather protection. It passed from the original owners to Crosville and later to Jersey Motor Transport where it completed its working life. It was subsequently rescued by enthusiasts and restored during the late 1960s in the original owners' livery. It is now in the care of Mr Hilditch, general manager of Halifax Corporation Passenger Transport Dept. Outings are limited, owing to a petrol consumption of some $4\frac{1}{2}$ miles per gallon.

1929 Chevrolet (USA/GB)
Series LQ

The Chevrolet LQ was produced in the USA during 1929 and was the company's first truck to have the famous six-cylinder valve-in-head engine. In Britain the 1929 LQ model was first assembled and later produced until the advent of the Bedford in 1931 (the first Bedford resembling the 1931 Chevrolet truck), hence the existence of '1929 Chevrolets' built in 1930 and 1931. This beautifully-restored example of an All-Weather coach is based on this chassis and spent its working life in Norfolk, where the canvas-topped body was originally produced by Bush & Twiddy. During 1962–3 it was completely reconditioned and refurbished after having been purchased by the well-known coach-operating firm of Charles W. Banfield Ltd of Peckham, London.

1929 Fiat (I)
603S

Similar to a British charabanc, this Italian equivalent was known as the Fiat 'Torpedone'. The folding top could be fully or half erected, as shown. The 603S chassis was available from 1925 until 1929 and had a $3\frac{1}{2}$-litre six-cylinder petrol engine with high-tension magneto ignition and a power output of 46 bhp at 2400 rpm. Wheelbase was 4.65 metres, tyre size 855×155, with a maximum load of 23 persons the bus had a maximum speed of 40 mph.

1929 Tatra (CS) T23

The Tatra 23 was a forward-control 4-ton chassis used mainly for truck, but occasionally also for bus, bodywork. Like other Tatras, it had a tubular chassis backbone with swing axles, providing independent front and rear wheel suspension. The engine was a water-cooled overhead-valve petrol four-cylinder of large cubic capacity: 7.48 litres. It produced 65 bhp at 1200 rpm and drove the rear axle shafts via a multi-disc clutch, a four-speed gearbox and a final-drive arrangement without universal joints. The Simplex spoke wheels were shod with large (40×10.5 inch) pneumatic tyres and the foot brake acted mechanically on all four wheels and on an extension of the propeller shaft. The bus body shown had longitudinal seats for 20 passengers and room for 20 standing.

1930 AEC (GB)
661 'Regent' Mk I

The AEC 'Regent' was another double-decker bus of which large numbers were produced. In fact the grand total was 7892, delivered during the period 1929 to 1947. The bus shown was one of a series of 42 supplied to the East Surrey Traction Company in 1929–30. They had 48-seater bodies, produced by Messrs Ransomes of Ipswich, and were easily identified by their square cabs and small front indicators. Similar buses were operated by East Surrey's Kentish equivalent, Autocar of Tunbridge Wells (both these undertakings had been acquired by the LGOC in June, 1929) and by the LGOC themselves ('ST'-Type).

1930 BMMO/SOS (GB)
IM4

BMMO passenger chassis were produced by the Birmingham & Midland Motor Omnibus Company, usually referred to as Midland Red. The letters SOS stood for Shire's Own Specification (Mr L. G. Wyndham Shire was BMMO's chief engineer). The engine, also produced by BMMO, was a four-cylinder petrol unit, the bodywork was by Short and seated 34 persons. The IM4 was in production until 1933 and the vehicle shown had fleet number 1163. Behind it is a BMMO M-type of the late 1920s. BMMO buses of various types were built also for associated companies, namely Trent and Northern General.

1930 Büssing (D)
VI GLn Dreiachser

This heavy six-wheeled tandem-drive Büssing chassis was used for bus and truck applications during the late 1920s. Buses using this chassis as a basis were of single- and double-decker configuration. The single-deckers shown here were operated by the City of Wiesbaden and embodied front entrance and rear exit doors of the jack-knife type. Note the location of the front axle in relation to the engine, a typical feature of German heavy commercial vehicles of the period. Like most six-wheeled passenger vehicles they had single tyres all round. Either a 90 or 110 bhp six-cylinder petrol engine could be fitted, driving by a four-speed gearbox, air brakes operated on the four rear wheels. Overall length was 10.2 metres, wheelbase 5.60+1.25 metres. They were produced between 1928 and 1934.

1930 Karrier (GB)
'Road-Rail'

This unorthodox 'Road-Railer' bus was one of a few vehicles produced by Karrier for operation on roads and rails. It was supplied in 1930 to the RTM (Rotterdamse Tramweg Maatschappij) in Rotterdam, Netherlands. The flanged wheels just inside the road wheels are clearly visible. They were used on the RTM's narrow-gauge tramway system. The prototype had also been a bus, namely a 26-seater (with forward-control) built for the British LMS. The second application was a goods vehicle. The RTM bus shown was the third and final model.

TRAM
ROTTERDAM
KARRIER
ROAD-RAIL
H·68729

1930 Magirus (D)
MM4

A typical German bus of the early 1930s, this Magirus model had a low chassis frame (introduced on the Magirus MM3 of 1927) and steel bodywork, also by Magirus. The engine was a V-12 cylinder petrol unit with a maximum power output of 100 bhp, supplied by the famous firm of Maybach. It provided a maximum speed of 60 mph, a noteworthy achievement in those pre-*Autobahn* days. The bus, which was delivered in September 1930, had a driver-operated folding door and a rear emergency exit door, both on the right-hand side. The seats were upholstered with leather.

1930 MAN (D)
6-ton/bus

A certain Mr Wachter of Spaichingen in Germany was one of a number of operators of a convertible vehicle. This 6-ton MAN chassis/cab could be used with either a truck body with dropsides and tilt or 29-seater bus body with front entrance and folding roof. Both bodies are shown here. Note the fancy rear wheel covers with embossed 'spokes', the ungainly strengthening rods between the front end of the chassis and the cab bulkhead and the transparent inserts in the truck body's tilt.

1930 Mercedes-Benz (D)
N46

The Mercedes-Benz N46 was a low-frame variant of the 2½-ton L45 truck, introduced in 1929. It was intended for a bodywork for 16 to 20 passengers. Both the L45 and the N46 were powered by a 50 bhp six-cylinder petrol engine, Model M16. The illustration shows the first all-enclosed sight-seeing coach with steel bodywork and sliding roof produced on this chassis by Karl Kässbohrer of Ulm/Donau. The coach was operated by Auto-Rundfahrten F. Schindele of Bad Wörishofen, south-east of Ulm. Other bus chassis produced by Daimler-Benz AG at this time included the N1 (13—16 pass.), N2 (26 pass.) and N56 (50 pass. six-wheeler).

1931 AEC (GB)
663 'Renown' LT

The Model 663 'Renown' was designed as a six-wheeler double-decker and was in production from 1929 until 1937 during which period a total of 1250 was built. Early models (in London) had an open staircase, later versions had enclosed staircases and rear platforms as shown. The first orders for the 'Renown' came from the LGOC, who designated it the 'LT'-Type. They ordered over 500 vehicles, and this plus additional orders from them and from other companies made AEC the largest British producer of six-wheeled passenger chassis in 1931. The first of London's trolleybuses, the 'Diddlers' as they came to be known, were based on a similar chassis and went into service in 1933. Also known as 'Renown' was the AEC Model 664, a variant for 30-foot single- and double-deckers (1930–9).

1931 Bedford (GB)
WHB

This Bedford Model WHB was the first purpose-built bus produced by Vauxhall Motors in Luton, in 1931. It had a 131-inch wheelbase, modified 2-ton truck chassis and was intended for 14-seater coachwork as shown. More common was the 157-inch wheelbase variant, Model WLB. The engine, in both cases, was a 26.3 hp overhead-valve six-cylinder, as fitted in contemporary Bedford trucks. The design was very similar to the American Chevrolet, which, in its 1929 LQ form, had been produced by Vauxhall before the advent of the Bedford range. The 1931 Bedford resembled the 1931 model Chevrolet. The vehicle illustrated has survived and is now owned by Arlington Motors.

1931 Daimler (GB)
COG 5 SD

This Daimler 35-seater 'Service Omnibus' was operated during the 1930s by Crosville Motor Services of Chester. The bodywork, designated Type B, was produced by United, an outgrowth of the United Automobile Services, itself a passenger transport enterprise formed in 1912. After World War I, United had started building bus bodies for their own use and from 1931 they sold bodies to other bus operators. In the July of that year the manufacturing interests of United were acquired by the Eastern Counties Omnibus Co. and five years later they became a separate company under the title of Eastern Coach Works Ltd.

1931 Dodge (USA/GB)
UF30A

F. C. Owen of Windsor was a 'jitney'-type operator using three vehicles with 14-seater bodies (a Bean, a Dodge and a Morris-Commercial). The Dodge is shown here, after the company was taken over by the London Passenger Transport Board. In Owen's service, it operated on the Windsor–Slough–Farnham Royal route. Dodge truck and bus chassis were produced by Graham Bros in the USA, utilizing Dodge mechanical components; in Britain they were assembled at Kew, especially the 30-cwt type, which was used with either a truck or bus bodywork.

1931 Reo (USA)
Six

An English-bodied 'Pullman' coach with 26 seats and folding canvas top; the bodywork was produced by H. E. Taylor of Norwich, under the trade name Eaton, and the vehicle was used on coach tours from Cromer in Norfolk for many years. It was then stored in the owner's garage for seven years until purchased for preservation in 1961 by the Historic Commercial Vehicle Club. It is shown here during preparations for the start of the annual HCVC London-to-Brighton Run in May 1965, when it was entered by the Best Bros of Hockley, Essex. Reo was one of the many imported makes in Britain during the 1920s and 1930s. Many were used as buses and coaches as there were no domestic chassis comparable for lightness and power and therefore for speed.

1931 Tatra (CS)
T27

Like the earlier Tatra 23, this 20-seater bus was based on a petrol-engined truck chassis. The payload was 3 tons. The chassis was of the tubular backbone type, bolted at the front to the engine/gearbox assembly and at the rear to the final drive/differential unit, enclosing the propeller shaft. The axles were of the swing type, front and rear, and the tyres were size 36×8, single all round. The engine was a 4260 cc water-cooled, four-cylinder, overhead-valve, petrol unit, developing 52 bhp at 2100 rpm, driving through a four-speed gearbox. The T27 was in production throughout the 1930s, during which period many modifications and improvements were made. There was also a 55 bhp six-wheeled variant, the T28, with bodywork for 28 seated passengers and 16 standing.

1932 Fiat (I)
635R

The Fiat 635R bus chassis was available during 1932–4 and is shown here with bodywork for 51 passengers. Wheelbase and overall length were 4.70 and 7.68 metres respectively and the 75 bhp six-cylinder 6220 cc petrol engine was good for 40 mph. The mechanical all-wheel brakes were vacuum servo-assisted. The tyre size was 9.00–20 and it weighed 9420 kg.

1932 Mercedes-Benz (D)

O4000

This was a 36-passenger sight-seeing coach with observation windows, folding roof and roof luggage rack, produced by Karl Kässbohrer on a Mercedes-Benz O4000 bus chassis. This chassis was introduced in 1929, superseding the earlier Model N2. The O4000 was derived from the contemporary L4000 4-ton truck chassis but instead of the truck's 7.07-litre, 70 bhp M26 engine it was powered by a 7.8-litre M37F of 110 bhp at 2000 rpm. Alternatively the bus chassis could be supplied with a 95 bhp Model OM5S diesel engine. All these engines had six cylinders. The O4000 was intended for coachwork for up to 42 passengers.

1933 Brush-Thornycroft (GB)
Trolleybus

In 1932 Bournemouth Corporation decided to replace their trams with a more modern and efficient transport system. Impressed with the merits of the trolleybus and already having a well-equipped generating system with miles of underground cable and overhead equipment for the trams, they decided to try the smooth and silent trolleybus on one of their existing tramway routes. Three different makes were used for the experiment, including this 32-seater supplied, on hire, by the Brush Electrical Engineering Co. Ltd and John I. Thornycroft & Co. Ltd, the joint manufacturers. As a result of the tests, however, it was decided to standardize Sunbeam-BTH six-wheeled double-saloon vehicles. The first order was for 12, but before the end of 1933 over 100 were on order.

1933 Karrier (GB)
E6 Trolleybus

Before World War II, Karrier Motors Ltd in Huddersfield, Yorkshire, were important manufacturers of trolleybuses for domestic and overseas customers. This E6 double-decker was supplied to Huddersfield Corporation Tramways, Karrier's 'hometown'. Both four- and six-wheeled models were produced with various types of bodywork. Karrier commenced production of trolleybuses in 1928 after having played a leading role in popularizing six-wheeled chassis for goods and passenger vehicles.

1933 Renault-Scemia (F)
TN6A

Louis Renault was the most important supplier of Paris city buses. This is a typical example of such a Paris bus, featuring an open rear platform to the wooden body, with the entrance centrally at the back, inside there is accommodation for 33 seated passengers. The petrol engine drives the rear axle and is located under the driver's seat. This specimen was in service from November 1933 until the spring of 1967 when it was purchased for preservation by Mr A. E. Adams of Adams Bristow Ltd, Kingston-on-Thames, Surrey. It was driven there from Paris under its own power. Scemia was involved in the production of Paris buses during the 1920s (with Schneider) but was later acquired by Renault.

1934 AEC (GB)
761 'Q'-Type

The AEC 'Q'-Type double-decker was a revolutionary side-engined model, introduced in 1933 and discontinued in 1935. Shown is Q5 of the London Transport Board, the 17th 'Q'-Type produced and the second to have a centre entrance. The body was by Weymann and had 62 seats. The engine, a six-cylinder petrol unit of 120 bhp, was placed behind the right-hand front wheel and drove the rear axle through a fluid coupling and a preselective four-speed gearbox. Only 23 were produced in this form. There were 318 of its companion, the 38-seater Model 762 single-decker, built during 1932–8. The 'Q' could also be supplied as a trolleybus. In the latter the power unit and gearbox were replaced by an 80 hp English Electric motor.

1934 Bedford (GB)
WTL

In 1934 Vauxhall Motors introduced a new range of semi-forward control Bedford 3-ton chassis and the long-wheelbase WTL was widely used for the mounting of bus and coach bodywork. A sun-roof coach by Duple Bodies & Motors Ltd of London is illustrated that was built for operation in Scotland. The chassis was designed for the transport of goods but only a few slight alterations were necessary to make it conform with the MOT regulations for the carriage of passengers. A typical Duple-bodied 20-seater coach with de luxe seating sold at £669 10s.

1934 Commer (GB)
'Centaur' B3

This attractive well-proportioned bus on Commer's 'Centaur' chassis, was operated by Imperial Airways in Khartoum, the capital of Sudan. It was delivered new in November 1934. The bodywork was produced by Weymann, one of the famous and old-established coachbuilders in England. Note the two rotating fresh-air extractor vents on the roof and the multiple air intake louvres above the side windows. The bus had left-hand drive and ample luggage accommodation at the rear.

1934 Fiat (I)
621R

Smartly styled this little Fiat coach could carry 18 persons at a speed of over 30 mph. It was propelled by a 45 bhp six-cylinder engine of 2½-litre capacity, driven through a multi-disc clutch and a four-speed gearbox and stopped by mechanical brakes on all wheels. Wheelbase and overall length were 3.80 and 5.83 metres respectively. 30×5 Michelin tyres were fitted with duals at rear. The 621R was produced between 1930 and 1934.

1934 SD (GB)

'Freighter'

By the mid 1930s, the old-established Shelvoke & Drewry 'Freighter' had been fitted with pneumatic tyres with duals at rear. Basically it was still the successful low-loading vehicle, popular with many municipalities for dustcarts. This particular vehicle, with bus body by Harrington, operated in Worthing, Sussex, and was powered by a 3-litre four-cylinder side-valve petrol engine, located transversally ahead of the front axle. There was provision for starting the engine by hand with a cranking handle from either side of the vehicle. Apart from a windscreen and roof the driver's compartment was entirely open.

1935 AEC (GB)

'STL'-Type

The 'STL'-Type was a long-wheelbase 60-seater and was also the last double-decker to be designed by the London General Omnibus Company (LGOC). It was in production when the London Passenger Transport Board (LPTB) was formed. A variation of the 'STL' with front entrance and 52 seats is shown. It was one of a series of 89 produced (fleet numbers STL 959–1043 and STL 1056–1059) during 1935. The bodywork was made at Chiswick. A further batch of 50 were bodied by Weymann of Addlestone in 1936 and one of these, which had been converted to a tree-lopper, has been rescued by a member of the London Bus Preservation Group.

1935 Leyland (GB)
TS7

This was one of seven 35-seater single-deckers delivered to East Midland in the mid 1930s. The cab was of the 'half-forward' type and the bodywork was manufactured by Eastern Coach Works of Lowestoft. It was typical of many vehicles bodied by ECW and other firms supplying the members of the BET group of companies. Note the double quarter bumpers at the rear and the low position of the handle of the emergency exit door behind the driver. The serial numbers allocated by Eastern Coach Works to this batch of bodies was 6531—7.

1936 Karrier (GB)
Trolleybus

In addition to six-wheeled models, Karrier Motors Ltd offered four-wheeled trolleybuses and a typical example is shown here. It had a 56-seater rear-entrance bodywork by Weymann and was supplied to the Borough of South Shields, County Durham in 1936. The unladen weight of this model was 6 tons 17 cwt. Karrier Motors Ltd were acquired by the Rootes Group and truck production was transferred from Huddersfield to Luton, Bedfordshire in 1934. Trolleybus production was moved to the Sunbeam works in Wolverhampton, which were also owned by the Rootes Group.

1936 Kässbohrer (D)
Sattelomnibus

Claimed by Kässbohrer to be the largest passenger vehicle of pre-war years, this tandem axle semi-trailer bus was 18.5 metres or over 60 ft long, including the tractor. It offered accommodation for no fewer than 170 passengers and featured sliding entrance/exit doors, two folding roof sections and a roof luggage rack. The bus-part being 'rigid' and resting on the 'fifth wheel' of a tractor truck (or truck-tractor), in this case a diesel-engined Mercedes-Benz; this type of bus should not be confused with an articulated bus. Note the triangle on the cab roof; when erected, as shown, this indicated that a (semi-) trailer was being towed.

1936 Magirus (D)
M65

In the spring of 1936 the German firm of C. D. Magirus AG in Ulm/Donau announced their first forward-control bus. It had a forward-mounted underfloor diesel engine of 150 hp with 12 horizontally-opposed cylinders. The slightly rounded contours of the all-metal bodywork gave the snoutless bus a pleasing and efficient appearance. On the front it carried the well-known Magirus emblem which combined the letter 'M' with a symbol of the Cathedral of Ulm. C. D. Magirus AG had merged with the Humboldt-Deutz-Motoren AG of Cologne in the previous year and in 1938 Klöckner-Humboldt-Deutz AG was founded. The bus shown went to Zittau in Saxony.

1936 Praga (CS)
TN

A heavy-duty petrol-engined bus chassis produced by the well-known Czech engineering firm of Ceskomoravska-Kolben-Danek AS of Prague-Lieben. The TN, which was in production throughout most of the 1930s, was a 3½-ton (payload) chassis, available with 5.20 and 5.80-metre wheelbase and bodywork for 22–35 and 25–40 seats respectively. In addition there was room for about 30 standing. The engine was a water-cooled petrol unit of 7085 cc cubic capacity (100×150 mm bore and stroke), developing 80 bhp at 1600 rpm. The fuel consumption was about 4 mpg and the maximum speed was 38 mph. Note the semaphore type direction indicators and the sturdy bumper-bar, mounted at an unusually high level.

1936 Thornycroft (GB)
'Daring' DD/RC6

Southampton Corporation Motor Service operated Thornycroft double-deckers for many years. An example of a petrol-engined 'Daring' is illustrated. This chassis was first produced in 1932, together with the 'Cygnet' single-decker chassis, and both remained the standard types for these applications in Thornycroft's range until civilian passenger vehicle production was suspended for World War II. It was about 1933 that the Thornycroft company began to adopt class names for most of their vehicles, in addition to the usual initials. Typical examples in the goods vehicle range were 'Speedy', 'Strenuous', 'Taurus', 'Dreadnought', etc. The 'Daring' had a 92 bhp six-cylinder petrol engine and had a wheelbase of 15 ft 11 in. It was designed for 52- to 56-seater bodies. A diesel engine version was also available.

1937 Büssing-NAG (D)
'Trambus'

When Hitler's Germany built its vast network of *Autobahnen* (motorways) during the 1930s it had an immediate effect on vehicle design for obvious reasons. Engines and chassis had to be able to withstand continuous high-speed operation and it was not long before coachbuilders introduced various degrees of streamlining, not only for appearance but to reduce drag as a result of wind resistance. Shown is a typical Kässbohrer-built *Stromlinien-Omnibus* of the 'Trambus'-type, operated by a Munich firm and based on a Büssing-NAG forward-control bus chassis. Note the large glass area and the folding roof.

1937 Opel (D)

'Blitz'

Mechanically the Opel 'Blitz' resembled its American and British General Motors cousins, the Chevrolet and the Bedford. In 1937 Opel introduced a special bus chassis for bodies for 26 to 29 seats or special bodies requiring a low and long chassis. Notable features were four full-width outrigger-type chassis cross members, welded on to the longitudinals and a five-speed gearbox. These luxury folding-top touring buses were bodied by Kässbohrer in Ulm/Donau, where the picture was taken.

1937 Praga (CS)

TOV

The Praga Model TOV was a three-axle tandem-drive bus chassis, powered by a 120 bhp water-cooled petrol engine. It had a carrying capacity of 8.7 tons and appeared with conventional as well as streamlined coachwork. An example of the latter, operated by the City of Prague, is illustrated here. The TOV was in production from about 1935 until World War II. Like all contemporary Czech vehicles, it had right-hand drive because until the War the rule of the road in Czechoslovakia was 'Drive on the Left'. The TOV had air brakes and a typical body would have accommodation for 28 seated persons and 16 standing.

1937 Renault-Scemia (F)

50-seater

In 1937 the *Société des Transports en Commun de la Region Parisienne* (TCRP) or Paris Public Transport Company, disposed of all their remaining trams and extended their fleet of buses. By the summer of 1937 there were 2682 50-seaters and 1369 26- and 48-seaters. Apart from 50 Panhard-Levassors and a few hundred of the famous old C.V. Schneider-type, all were Renault-Scemias. Early types had an open rear platform but a new type (as shown, still going strong in the late 1960s) was taken into service for suburban service, featuring an enclosed rear platform and a side entrance. The original version still had open sides to the cab. The steering wheel was on the left, rather than in the centre as on very early Paris buses.

1937 SD (GB)

'Freighter'

Crosville Motor Services of Chester were among the customers of SD 'Freighter'-based passenger vehicles. This so-called 'Toastrack' was taken into service in 1937. It was an open-sided 32-seater with eight rows of seats. Earlier, Crosville had used similar 'hardtop charabancs' with tram-type tiller controls. Southdown Motor Services Ltd of Brighton used the SD chassis with a normal bus body with central entrance/exit and the engine placed at the rear, unlike the model shown which had the power unit mounted transversally under the driver's seat.

1937 Thornycroft (GB)
'Amazon'

The Thornycroft 'Amazon' was a 6-ton six-wheeled tandem-drive (6×4) truck chassis, powered by a six-cylinder direct injection diesel engine of 7.88 litres cubic capacity and developing a maximum output of 100 bhp. Bolted to the four-speed main gearbox was a two-speed auxiliary unit providing a low range of gears to enable the vehicle to negotiate difficult terrain. The 'Amazon' was operated in various parts of the world, not only for the carrying of goods but also for passenger transport, notable examples being the high-speed coaches operated by the Iraq State Railway. This stylish 26-seater bus for long-distance desert service was one of them and was exhibited at the London Motor Show before being delivered.

1938 Büssing-NAG (D)
650N

A typical Büssing-NAG chassis of the late 1930s powered by a 13½-litre six-cylinder diesel engine with a power output of 135–145 bhp. This engine had two blocks of three cylinders, a seven-bearing crankshaft, pre-combustion chambers and 17:1 compression ratio. Injection and electrical equipment was all by Bosch. This bus was operated by the City of Brunswick (Braunschweig), where the Büssing works were, and still are, situated. Note the long front overhang, the flexible connection between bonnet and bulkhead, and the high position of the steering wheel, typical features of many German heavy vehicles of the period. Brakes were air-over-hydraulic, on all wheels. Overall length was 9.64 or 10.24 metres, wheelbase 5.40 or 6.00 metres respectively. Production period was from 1936 to 1940.

1938 Sunbeam-BTH (GB)
MF2 Trolleybus

The City of Durban in South Africa purchased its first fleet of Sunbeam trolleybuses in 1934 and subsequently placed several repeat orders. This illustration shows one of a fleet of 60-seater double-deckers delivered for service in Durban about 1938. At this time Sunbeam Commercial Vehicles Ltd of Moorfield Works, Wolverhampton, offered six trolleybus chassis, namely the MF1 for 32–4 passengers, the MF2 and MF2A for 48–54 passengers, the MF3 and MF3A lightweights for 24 passengers and the MS2 for 60–70 passengers. The last named model was a six-wheeler and had a 95 bhp motor, the others were four-wheelers with 80 bhp motor. All models had BTH electrical equipment.

1939 Leyland (GB)
'Cub'

This Leyland 'Cub' is believed to be the only surviving example of London Transport's 'CR' class, which represented the first rear engine design to be put into quantity production. The 'CR' class comprised 49 buses, all of which were put into storage during the war years because of a shortage of spares. After the war they reappeared on 'Relief' and other special duties. They were eventually withdrawn in 1952 and some found their way to Cyprus and Ceylon. Number CR14, illustrated here, spent some time with the Museum of British Transport in Clapham, London and in 1967 was purchased by enthusiasts for preservation. In May 1971 it appeared in the annual London-to-Brighton Run of the Historic Commercial Vehicle Club, after restoration work had been carried out to engine and bodywork.

1939 Magirus (D)
L145

This Magirus L145 was made for the *Deutsche Reichspost* and featured standardized bodywork produced to their specification. It was powered by a 125 bhp water-cooled Deutz F6M516 six-cylinder diesel engine of 9.1 litres cubic capacity. Since the merger with Humboldt-Deutz, Magirus increased their use of Deutz diesel engines for their trucks and buses. In this application the engine drove through a separately mounted ZF gearbox with four forward speeds plus a *Schnellgang* (overdrive). The weight of this bus was approximately 7500 kg.

1939 Opel (D)
'Blitz'

The Adam Opel AG of Rüsselsheim/Main, General Motors' German subsidiary, produced a special 4.65 metre wheelbase bus chassis in their successful range of 'Blitz' commercial vehicles. It was widely used in Germany and exported to many other countries, including Great Britain where it was introduced in 1937 and sold at £295 (or complete with 26-seater coach bodywork by Strachans (Successors) Ltd for £850). The example shown was one of many operated in the Netherlands where Opels were and are very popular. It is fitted with a Dutch 29-seater body. The chassis remained in production until the end of the war and was co-produced by Daimler-Benz. The engine was a 3.6-litre overhead-valve, petrol six-cylinder, much like that of the American Chevrolet and British Bedford.

1939 Sunbeam-BTH (GB)
MS2 Trolleybus

In addition to Durban, the South African Cities of Cape Town, Johannesburg and Pretoria used Sunbeam trolleybuses. One of the large fleet operated by Cape Town Tramways is shown, which included 71 six-wheelers. All these vehicles were fitted with BTH electric traction equipment. The motor was a 95 bhp compound-wound field type, arranged for regenerative and rheostatic braking (Ransomes system). It was carried on a subframe, flexibly mounted at four points and easily removable as an assembly. The master controller was combined with a reverser and Sunbeam-Lockheed hydraulic brakes actuated on all wheels. The rear bogie featured twin-spring suspension. After the war more Sunbeam vehicles were supplied to Cape Town.

1942 Commer (GB)
'Superpoise' Q4

Commer 'Superpoise' diesel-engined (P6) tractor truck with bus-type 38-seater semi-trailer, supplied in 1942. It was claimed to be the first one of its type licenced in England and two were operated by the Mansfield & District Traction Company of Mansfield, Nottinghamshire. In 1944 they were passed on to the Nottinghamshire and Derby Traction Company. Most of Commer's wartime production was for the war effort but a limited number of commercial trucks was built and supplied for essential civilian use. Note the wartime blackout features, the 'lifeguards' (wooden slats between the wheels) and the vehicle width indicators bolted to the front wings. The RAF employed similar tractor units to tow 'Queen Mary' aircraft transporter semi-trailers, in addition to the more common forward-control Model Q2.

1945 Bedford (GB)
OB, OWB

The Bedford OB was introduced in 1939 and continued until 1948 with the exception of the war years during which an austere version, designated OWB, was produced. The OB was the bus chassis in Vauxhall's Bedford 'O'-Series, which also included the OS and OL truck chassis. The OB had a 174-inch wheelbase, six-cylinder, overhead-valve engine rated at 27.3 hp, four-speed gearbox and servo-assisted hydraulic brakes. The specimen shown was operated by the Royal Air Force. The additional bumper bars and the front wheel hub covers were a feature of Bedford bus chassis. Some of the wartime OWBs were less austere than others and these were referred to as having a 'relaxed' specification.

1945 Vetra (F)
CS60R

Immediately after World War II, the *Société des Véhicules et Tracteurs Electriques* (VETRA) in Paris recommenced production of several types of trolleybuses, both four- and six-wheeled. The CS60R was designed for 60 passengers and had a cruising speed of just over 30 mph. It was of integral chassisless construction and featured a Renault-Scemia rear axle. The motor was mounted amidships. Overall length was 9.06 metres, the wheelbase 5 metres. Empty, the bus weighed about 7 tons; with 60 passengers and crew of two the total weight was about $11\frac{1}{2}$ tons.

1946 Bristol (GB)
L

The Bristol Tramways & Carriage Company Ltd of Filton, Bristol, was founded in 1908, and in 1938 became a member of the Tilling Group. In 1947 the company was nationalized and began to produce buses and trucks exclusively for nationalized operating companies. The majority of vehicles produced were PSVs. Illustrated is a Bristol Model L stage carriage single-decker, bodied by Eastern Coach Works Ltd of Lowestoft (Body No. 1245), for operation in Bristol. The unladen weight of this bus was just under $6\frac{1}{2}$ tons.

1947 Commer (GB)
'Superpoise' QD353

One of the two Commer 'Superpoise' Model QD353 diesel buses operated by Devilprased Motors of Calicut, Malabar, on the west coast of the Madras province in South India. The chassis/scuttles were supplied by Messrs Simpson & Co. Ltd of Madras. The bodywork was produced locally and was a simple design with no side windows and of composite construction. Normally the Commer 'Superpoise' was powered by the same basic six-cylinder, side-valve petrol engine that powered various Humber and Karrier models (like Commer products of the Rootes Group) but these buses had the optional Perkins P6 six-cylinder diesel engine.

1947 Fiat (I)
626RNL

Fiat's Model 626RNL passenger vehicle chassis was derived from the 626NL truck and was first introduced just before the war, in 1939. The letter 'N' in the model designation indicated *Nafta* or diesel. The Model 326 diesel engine was a 70 bhp 5.75-litre six-cylinder, driving through a five-speed gearbox and good for a maximum speed of 45 mph. The wheelbase was 4.05 metres, the overall length was 7.90 metres. The 626RNL is illustrated here with a 28-seater coach bodywork.

1948 Bedford (GB)
OWB

This 29-seater luxury coach was produced in 1948 by Bonallack for Mountain
Services Ltd of Chelsea, London. It was
based on a 174-inch wheelbase Model
OWB chassis which was entirely reconditioned and rebuilt. The radiator grille
was made by the bodybuilders and
resembled the civilian type grille. The
bonnet was military pattern but modified
and the headlamps were mounted on
stalks, strengthened with a tiebar. Note
the narrow sliding side door. The engine
was the Bedford 3.5-litre, overhead-
valve Six, developing 72 bhp.

1948 Thornycroft (GB)
SG/NR6

One of five 33-seater coaches delivered to the Bristol Co-operative Society Ltd, fitted with bodywork by Longwell Green Coachworks Ltd, also of Bristol. Among the noteworthy features of these coaches were a synchromesh and preselective mechanism adapted to the higher ratios of the gearbox and a steering wheel which was adjustable for height. The engine was a 7.88-litre 100 bhp six-cylinder diesel. Two levers were provided in the cab for gear selection; one, located on the left, for engaging reverse, first, second and 'locked' second positions, the other, mounted on the steering column, was for preselective engagements of second, third and fourth. For normal driving only the latter lever was used, the hydraulic coupling permitting the vehicle to start in second gear on level ground.

1949 Albion (GB)
'Viking'

Swallow Coaches of St Pauls Road, Smethwick, Staffordshire, took delivery of this smart 'fully-fronted' coach in 1949. Unlike many other coaches on the Albion chassis, this specimen did not have the exposed, classic, pre-war style, Albion radiator. Instead it was hidden behind the front end panelling which incorporated a more modern radiator grille design. The 'Viking' had a 120 bhp six-cylinder diesel engine with four-speed gearbox. Albion also offered 'Victor' and 'Valkyrie' passenger chassis for 26–33 and 35–40 passengers respectively. These had four-cylinder oil engines although the 'Victor' could be supplied with an alternative six-cylinder petrol power unit.

1949 Volkswagen (D)
Eight-seater

In 1949 Volkswagenwerk introduced their commercial models, aptly named *Transporter*. Like the Volkswagen car, later known as the 'Beetle', the *Transporter* range became tremendously successful and also a trendsetter. From the start there were closed van and 8-seater bus versions and other models, e.g. a pickup, were added. Like the car, they had an air-cooled horizontally-opposed engine, mounted at the rear. In order to obtain more ground clearance the rear axle halves, which were of the 'swinging' type, had drop-gear final drives at their ends which at the same time provided a further gear reduction. According to one British trade journal, the bus did not offer any degree of comfort. This, however, was soon rectified and later models were much better equipped and finished.

1950 AEC (GB)
'Regal' Mk III

This fine coach, operated by Surrey Motors Ltd of Sutton, Surrey, was a typical example of the final development of the AEC 'Regal' chassis which had been in continuous production since 1929 (except for interruption of the war years). By this date the modern underfloor-engined coach had made its appearance and, apart from a few hundred vehicles of the out-dated type produced during 1950–1, no more half-cab vehicles were produced for use as coaches. The bodywork shown was a 33-seater by Harrington and the unladen weight of the complete vehicle was just under 7 tons.

1950 Commer (GB)
'Avenger'

One of a fleet of Commer 'Avenger' passenger chassis fitted with special, locally built observation bus bodywork for Australian National Airways. Painted in the Airways colour scheme of silver and light blue the buses were used to meet the 44-passenger ANA 'Skymasters' at Essendon Airport and transport them to Melbourne. The upper deck had seating capacity for 18, the lower deck for 16, below the upper deck was a 150 cu. ft luggage compartment. The buses were 27 ft 6 in long, 10 ft 6 in high and 8 ft wide, the latest type of anti-draught window was installed.

1950 Karrier (GB)
'Avenger'

The Rootes Commer/Karrier 'Avenger' passenger chassis was introduced in 1949 and was powered by the makers' six-cylinder 109 bhp underfloor petrol engine. This engine was also used in contemporary Commer forward-control trucks. From 1954 the Rootes TS3 three-cylinder two-stroke diesel was optionally available. Illustrated is a 22-seater 'Luxury Liner' built on the 'Avenger' chassis by New Zealand Motor Bodies Ltd in Petone, for service in the North Island by Massey Motors in conjunction with Larsens Tours Ltd. Most 'Avengers' were sold under the Commer name.

1951 Commer (GB)
'Superpoise' Mk III

Commer 2—3-ton 'Superpoise' chassis with 22-seater bus body used by the Special Care Service of the Ireland Hospitals Authority for conveying school children to dental clinics and as a large emergency ambulance. Supplied by A. S. Baird Ltd of Belfast, it embodied seats running the full length of each side of the body which were quickly convertible into stretcher bases, whilst a wide rear door and folding step gave easy access for the vehicle when used as an ambulance. A folding door on the left-hand side was provided for passengers.

1951 Magirus-Deutz (D)

O6500H

This was one of the first forward-control rear-engined buses to be produced by the Magirus works of Klöckner-Humboldt-Deutz AG. The chassis was purpose-built for passenger vehicles, rather than an adaptation of a truck chassis. The model designation O6500H is explained as follows: O = *Omnibus*, 6500 = chassis payload rating (6500 kg), H = *Heckmotor* (rear engine). The engine was, naturally, an air-cooled Deutz unit and the large cooling air intake can be clearly seen on the roof at the rear. In this instance, it was a V-8-cylinder with an output of 175 bhp, driving through a ZF-Media transmission with electro-magnetic operation. The O6500H made its public début at the IAA international motor show in Frankfurt in 1951 and in 1953 a smaller version, the O3500H, was added, replacing the earlier normal-control O3500.

1952 Fiat (I)
642RN

A neatly styled coach with capacity for 44 persons plus 520 kg of luggage was this Fiat 642RN of the early 1950s. Its 92 bhp 6650-cc six-cylinder diesel power unit provided a maximum speed of almost 50 mph. Wheelbase and overall length were 4.90 and 8.99 metres respectively and the 20×8 wheels were shod with 9.00–20 tyres. Transmission was dual-range four-speed (8F2R) and the hydraulic brakes were air-assisted.

1953 Bristol (GB)
LD6G

Registered in late 1953 in Lindsey, Lincs, this double-decker, operated by the Lincolnshire Road Car Company, was typical of Bristols of the period, featuring a rather bulbous engine bonnet and jack knife type entry/exit doors at the rear. The bodywork was by Eastern Coach Works of Lowestoft and offered seating for a total of 58 passengers on the lower and upper decks. The engine was a Gardner six-cylinder diesel and the bus was known as 'Lodekka' because of its specially low overall height. These low models had a centre aisle, rather than the customary and inconvenient side gangway.

1953 Karrier (GB)
'Gamecock'

One of four school buses supplied in late 1953 to the Lanarkshire Education authorities by Messrs T. M. Erskin & Co, Karrier distributors in Renfrew, Scotland. They were based on the 3—4-ton 'Gamecock' chassis with 11 ft 9 in wheelbase and Rootes 85 bhp six-cylinder underfloor petrol engine, which also powered the Karrier 'Bantam'. This engine was well-known on account of its having porous chrome cylinder bores as a standard feature.

1954 AEC/MCW (GB)

'Regal' Mk IV

This type of bodywork was produced in large numbers by Metropolitan–Cammell–Weymann to the specification of the London Transport Executive. There were four variations: the Central Bus, the Country Bus, the Green Line Coach (shown) and the Private Hire Coach. The first two were 30 ft 41-seaters and identical except for the doors (Glider-type on Country Bus). The Green Line Bus had modified seating arrangement for 39 persons and was equipped with luggage racks. The Private Hire Coach was not unlike the Green Line Coach but shorter (27 ft 6 in; 35 seats) and was fitted with large observation windows in the coving of the roof. All models were 7 ft 6 in wide and 10 ft 5 in high (unladen).

1954 Commer (GB)
R741

Basic transport for the natives was provided by two Commer 7-ton long-wheelbase Model R741 truck chassis fitted with sturdy locally made bodywork and operated by Ojukwu Transport Ltd in Lagos, Nigeria. There were three seats in the cab (two for passengers) and no fewer than 48 in the main body. The vehicle weighed just under 4 tons and had a GVW (gross vehicle weight) rating of 11 tons. Note the roll-down side curtains.

1955 Beadle (GB)
'Rochester'

From 1955 until 1957 Messrs John C. Beadle (Coachbuilders) Limited of Lowfield Street, Dartford, Kent, produced integral-type buses and coaches under their own name. The firm already had several years of experience in building integral buses, utilizing pre-war mechanical components, for companies like Southdown, East Kent, etc. (1947–51). Illustrated is one of the first Beadles, a 41-seater front-entrance coach for the East Kent Road Car Company of Canterbury. It was powered by the Rootes TS3 diesel engine, driving through a four-speed gearbox. The other models Beadle offered were the 'Chatham', a 45-seater front-entrance bus, and the smaller petrol-engined 'Canterbury' 29-seater and 'Thanet' 32-seater. All had Rootes Group mechanical components.

1955 Commer (GB)

'Avenger'

Typical British lightweight bodywork of the 1950s, constructed by Messrs H. V. Burlingham Ltd of Blackpool, Lancashire, on a Commer 'Avenger' passenger chassis with Rootes TS3 three-cylinder two-stroke diesel engine. The coach had seating accommodation for 37 passengers and a wheelbase length of 17 ft 6 in. It was operated by Allenways Ltd of Moseley Road, Birmingham. The all-metal bodywork weighed 2 tons 6 cwt, the complete vehicle 5 tons 12 cwt. The design was known as 'Seagull'.

1955 Leyland (GB)
'Titan' PD2/13

The Leyland 'Titan' chassis was in production for many years and appeared with bodywork from most if not all the leading coachbuilders. Shown is No. 60 of the fleet of the County Borough of Bolton Transport Department, carrying a 1954 registration. The 58-seater bodywork, produced by Metro-Cammell, was of the high-bridge type. The 7-ton bus had accommodation for a total of 58 seated passengers, namely 31 in the upper saloon and 27 in the lower saloon. The engine was a six-cylinder Leyland diesel.

1956 Bristol (GB)
LS5G

This was a luxury coach produced by Eastern Coach Works Ltd of Lowestoft, Suffolk (Body No. 8940) based on the Bristol LS5G chassis in 1956. It was delivered to Eastern Counties, i.e. the Eastern Counties Omnibus Company Ltd, whose headquarters were in Norwich. The coach offered luxury accommodation for 32 passengers. Note the special kerb-view window in the front door. The engine was a Gardner diesel. Many hundreds of these coaches, with various seating capacities, were supplied to BTC operators during the period from 1952 to 1958.

1956 Karrier (GB)
'Bantam'

Two of these 21-seater personnel carriers, based on 122-inch wheelbase 'Bantam' chassis, were delivered to the Western Region of British Railways in 1956. The bodies were built by Commercial Motors (Harrow) Ltd and were equipped with five double semi-coach type seats on each side with an additional seat at the front left-hand side. Access was gained through a sliding door on the left and an emergency door was fitted at the rear. They were used 'for the mustering and dispersing of train crews operating a 24-hour service'.

1957 Commer (GB)
'Avenger'

A straightforward 43-seater bus, operated by Wansbeck Motor Services of Ashington, Northumberland. The body, built by Plaxtons (Scarborough) Ltd, was 30 ft long by 8 ft wide. The passenger entrance was a single folding type door, giving a clear width of 2 ft $3\frac{3}{4}$ in when open. A front-hung coach-type door was fitted as an emergency exit immediately opposite the passenger entrance. The bus was based on the diesel-engined Commer 'Avenger' chassis.

1957 Ford (GB)
'Thames Trader' 500E

In May 1957 the Ford Motor Company in England introduced the 'Thames Trader' FC (forward-control) series with choice of several engines. For the 5-ton vehicles, there were two petrol and two diesel engines available, the latter being the well-known four- and six-cylinder diesel Ford 4D and 6D. A medium-size coach is shown that was built by Messrs Thurgoods of Ware on the 'Thames Trader' chassis. In 1958, Ford introduced a purpose-built bus/coach chassis, with six-cylinder petrol or diesel engine. Known as the 'Thames' PSV, it had a 212-inch wheelbase.

1958 Commer (GB)
BFD 3023

This Commer 12-seater coach was supplied in early 1958 to Aerolineas Argentinas by Conde Barao Lda of Lisbon, the Commer-Karrier distributors in Portugal. The bodywork was a modification of the standard $1\frac{1}{2}$-ton Forward Control Mk V Van, carried out by Conde Barao Lda, and featured a large locker at the rear, with twin doors for luggage accommodation. The bus was powered by the four-cylinder Rootes light diesel engine.

1958 Daimler (GB)
CVG6

This 27-foot chassis was in production for many years. It was used for front- and rear-entrance double-deckers and the rear-entrance example shown was operated by Coventry Corporation Transport. The front end structure, incorporating front cover, bonnet top, wings, etc. was made in fibreglass. There was a choice of diesel engines: Daimler CD6 or Gardner 5LW or 6LW (later also 6LX). Transmission could be manual, semi- or fully-automatic, the latter of course being the Daimler fluid flywheel with electro-pneumatic four-speed epicyclic gearbox.

1959 Austin/Verheul (GB/NL)
33 Diesel

The chassis of this 23-seater Anglo—Dutch coach was a modification of the Austin K3-type truck chassis, executed by NV Auto-Industrie Verheul of Waddinxveen in the Netherlands, who also designed and built the coachwork. Overall length was 6.86 metres and the wheelbase was 3.50 metres. GVW was 6100 kg and the bus was powered by the BMC 3.4-litre four-cylinder diesel engine, driving through a four-speed gearbox. A 3.99-litre six-cylinder petrol engine could be supplied as an alternative. The bus was marketed by the Dutch Austin distributor Messrs R. J. Stokvis & Zonen NV in Rotterdam.

1959 Mercedes-Benz (D)
O317

The Mercedes-Benz O317 large-capacity city bus made its public début at the 1957 Frankfurt Motor Show. It had a capacity of 120 seated passengers, underfloor engine with either manual or hydraulic transmission, and pneumatic suspension. The power unit was similar to the OM326 which had proved itself in the L326 long-distance truck, a six-cylinder diesel with an output of 220 bhp (SAE). The O317 was claimed to be the first German bus with air suspension, a system which comprised two rubber bellows at the front and four at the rear, with height compensation control.

1960 Citroën (F)

T23

The Citroën 23 Series originated from before the war and, with periodical modifications and improvements, remained in production for many years. The chassis was designed for operation at a GVW of between 3500 and 5000 kg and many were used as the basis for medium-sized buses like the one shown here. They accommodated between 23 or 28 passengers, but school-buses were built with 48 seats. The wheelbase was 3.75 metres. The example shown has the standard truck-type radiator grille and was powered by a Perkins P4 four-cylinder diesel engine.

1960 Commer (GB)

'Avenger'

The 'Avenger' passenger chassis was widely used by various coachbuilders, including Duple Motor Bodies Ltd of Hendon, London. Shown here is a Duple 'Corinthian' coach, designed to accommodate 37 to 41 passengers. The wide windscreen embodied a single centre panel and two wrap-round quarter sections, all of compound curvature, quarter-inch, toughened safety-plate glass. The entrance door was of the outside-sliding type and in compliance with MoT requirements, there was an emergency exit in the rear window in addition to the emergency/driver's coach-type door on the right-hand side.

1960 DAF (NL)

TB160

The DAF Model TB160 passenger chassis was designed for the mounting of bus or coach bodywork with accommodation for 40 to 50 seated passengers or 70 to 80 seated and standing. It was available with either a 120 or 165 bhp six-cylinder diesel engine. Shown is a luxury touring coach operated by Touring Centrale Jacques van Dijk of Eindhoven and produced by NV Auto-Industrie Verheul of Waddinxveen (which was later taken over by Leyland).

1960 Ford (GB)

'Thames' PSV

In 1958 Ford of England introduced their first purpose-built 'Thames' PSV (Public Service Vehicle) chassis. Illustrated is a typical example of a service bus based on this chassis, made for export and photographed at the Ford Motor Co. plant at Dagenham, Essex. The coachwork was produced by Duple Motor Bodies Ltd. There were four 'Thames' PSV chassis, namely the 568E (RHD) and 569E (LHD) with Ford six-cylinder overhead-valve 4888 cc petrol engine and the 570E (RHD) and 571E (LHD) with Ford 6D six-cylinder 5416 cc diesel engine. All had 212-inch wheelbase.

1961 Commer (GB)
'Avenger'

Plaxtons (Scarborough) Limited offered this Commer-based 'Embassy' luxury coach, embodying a completely restyled exterior with a large, curved, Triplex, wrap-round, two-piece windscreen. Construction was of proven Plaxton composite type utilizing steel and aluminium alloy for the stressed member with hardwood filling. The side panels were aluminium with front and rear end panelled in fibreglass-reinforced plastic. There was accommodation for 41 passengers on Plaxton luxury seats. The coach shown was in service with Eddie Brown, a Yorkshire operator, and was supplied by Howdens of Harrogate.

1961 DAF (NL)
B1600

The DAF Model B1600 passenger vehicle chassis was derived from the contemporary, forward-control DAF Model A1600 truck chassis. A longer wheelbase was one of the obvious differences. It was designed to take bus and coach bodywork with either 40 to 48 seats or 60 to 70 seats and standing places. There was a choice of three power units: 120 or 165 bhp diesel or 155 bhp petrol engine. An export bus with right-hand drive is shown.

1961 Ford (GB)

'Thames' PSV

Duple Motor Bodies Ltd of Hendon, London, produced this attractive 'Yeoman' 41-passenger luxury coach body on the 'Thames' PSV (and other) chassis. It was of Duple composite lightweight construction featuring selected hard woods reinforced with steel and alloy and incorporating internal trussing where necessary. The exterior was panelled mainly in 16 and 18 gauge aluminium. The large windscreen had a special parallel tandem-type wiper, used to ensure the maximum clear area.

1961 Mercedes-Benz (D)

O321HL

The Mercedes-Benz O321HL (or H–L) was basically similar to the company's O321H but longer by one window length, or 417 as opposed to 367 inches. The floor area was 201 sq ft as compared with 167 sq ft. It had 41 seats in ten rows or, alternatively, 45 in eleven. The standard power unit was the six-cylinder OM321 diesel of 110 bhp (DIN, 120 SAE) but the more powerful OM322 could be installed on request (126 bhp DIN, 138 bhp SAE). The rear axle was driven through a five-speed gearbox. All Mercedes-Benz buses are produced in Daimler-Benz AG's Mannheim plant.

1962 Daimler (GB)
'Fleetline'

The low-height double-decker body on this Daimler 'Fleetline' rear-engined chassis was built by The Northern Counties Motor and Engineering Co. Ltd of Wigan for operation by Middlesbrough Corporation. The bus incorporated a step-free platform and wide staircase (behind the driver) with large circulating area on the upper deck, and was built to the low height of 13 ft 5 in with central aisle seating layout in both saloons. It weighed just under 9 tons. A feature of interest was the treatment of the rear end to produce a full-sided effect whilst retaining silence and good accessibility for engine removal.

1962 Ford (GB)
'Thames' PSV

The Duple 'Firefly' 37 to 41-seater luxury coach was an entirely new body design for the 41-seater capacity class, produced by Duple Motor Bodies (Northern) Ltd (formerly Burlingham) of Blackpool, Lancs. The body, originally designed by Burlingham, was of composite light-weight construction, the exterior panelling being a combination of fibreglass-reinforced plastic and aluminium. The layout embodied an outside sliding door behind the left-hand-side front wheel with emergency exits provided by coach-type doors opposite the main entrance beside the driver and behind the right-hand rear-wheel arch.

1962 Karrier (GB)
'Gamecock'

This 35-seater petrol-engined Karrier 'Gamecock' bus was produced in South Africa for the use of welfare organizations, institutions and orphanages and to transport elderly and infirm passengers in the Cape Peninsula on outings, picnics, etc. The project was conceived and carried out by the Lions Clubs and the 'Gamecock' chassis was chosen because of its low frame height, an obvious advantage for elderly people where easy entry and exit are of primary importance. The bus was supplied by Orpen Motors (Pty) Ltd of Cape Town.

1963 Fiat (I)
410

In production during 1962–3 was this 11-metre bus with accommodation for 88 passengers. It was powered by a 176 bhp Fiat 310H61 six-cylinder diesel engine of 11,548 cc, driving through a four-speed gearbox. Full air brakes were fitted, supplemented by auxiliary brakes acting on transmission and engine. The wheelbase was 5.40 metres and the tyre size was 6–20. The vehicle's maximum road speed was quoted as 32 mph.

1963 Škoda (CS)
706RTO

The Czech Škoda 706RTO was available for many years in three versions; a city transport bus, a long-distance bus and a luxury touring coach. A Karosa-bodied city bus is shown with front entrance and rear exit doors of the double pneumatically-operated type. The seats were of tubular construction with fibreglass pressings; driver's and conductor's seat were sprung and foam-rubber padded. There was accommodation for 28 sitting passengers and 22 standing. The engine was a Škoda six-cylinder 170 bhp diesel of 11.8-litre capacity. In addition to air service brakes, there was a mechanical handbrake and an engine brake.

1964 Bedford (GB)
VAL

The Bedford VAL was a twin-steer bus and coach chassis with a 131 bhp Leyland O400 diesel engine and five-speed overdrive gearbox, hydraulic service brakes with air-pressure servo assistance, mechanical parking brake operating on the two steering axles and an auxiliary brake operating independently on a drum-type transmission brake on the rear driving axle. The chassis cost £1,775 and is shown here with a 52-seater luxury coach bodywork by Plaxton.

1964 Dodge (USA)
S600

In 1962 the Dodge Division of the Crysler Corporation introduced their well-known 'D'-Series trucks, the front-end styling of which was later used on British-built Dodge Kew normal-control trucks. In the 'D'-Series were several school bus chassis, with wheelbase sizes varying from 157 to 258 inches. These had model designations with 'S' suffix, e.g. the S400 was the bus version of the D400 truck chassis. The S400 had a GVW rating of 15,000 lbs, the remaining models 22,000 lbs. A typical 'school bus' style body is shown utilized by the US Air Force in Britain (hence RHD and the entrance/exit door on left-hand side). It was a 37-passenger model.

1964 Ford (GB)
'Thames' PSV 674E

This 52-seater luxury lightweight coach was offered by Thomas Harrington of Hove, Sussex, on the 'Thames' 11-metre Model 674E (or 676E diesel) chassis. It was designated 'Legionnaire Mark II' and was introduced in September 1964 for the 1965 selling season. Of all metal construction, it measured 36 ft by 8 ft 2½ in and the unladen body weight was under 3 tons. The engine was either a Ford six-cylinder overhead-valve petrol with 4888 cc or a Ford six-cylinder diesel with 5416 cc capacity.

1964 Leyland (GB)
'90'

Displayed at the 1964 Commercial Motor Show in London, this new Leyland '90' model had an 18-seater personnel carrier bodywork produced by Cravens Homalloy. It was a long-wheelbase (11 ft 3 in) model, ordered by Messrs Steel, Peech and Tozer Ltd and was from a new range of Leyland medium truck chassis designed for a GVW of $4\frac{1}{2}$ tons. Features included a new four-cylinder 60 bhp Leyland Model OE.160 diesel engine, four-speed synchromesh gearbox and servo-assisted brakes.

1965 Fiat (I)
625 NP

This neat mid-size 19-seater was built on a 3.30-metre wheel-base chassis with four-cylinder 66 bhp 2.7-litre diesel engine. Overall dimensions were 6.35×2.10×2.47 metres and a maximum speed of 55 mph was possible. The tyres were 6.50—16 on 16×5.00E wheels and the brakes were hydraulic. The transmission comprised a single-plate clutch and a five-speed gearbox.

1965 Mazda (J)
AEVA(A)

The unusual styling was one of the features of this Mazda Light Bus offered by Toyo Kogyo Co. Ltd of Japan. It provided accommodation for 25 persons and weighed 2550 kg (GVW 3925 kg). The overall dimensions were 5.99 × 2.02 × 2.32 metres and the wheelbase was 3.09 metres. It had a 1985 cc four-cylinder petrol engine of 81 bhp, driven through a four-speed synchromesh gearbox and the maximum speed was 60 mph. The hydraulic brakes were assisted by a Bendix Hydromaster and hydraulic integral type power steering was an optional extra. It was offered on the Japanese home market for the equivalent of just over £1,650.

1965 Mercedes-Benz (D)
O302

In the mid 1960s, Daimler-Benz launched the Mannheim-built Mercedes-Benz O302 range of rear-engined passenger vehicles. There were three basic types, namely a touring coach, a country bus (*Überland-Omnibus* shown) and a city bus. There were variants of the latter with normal-height and high curved side windows. The latter were a feature also of the touring coach. In addition, there was a choice of three wheelbase sizes for each type, viz. 4.68, 5.05 and 5.85 metres, with overall lengths of 9.62, 10.15 and 10.95 metres respectively. These three variants were designated 10R, 11R and 12R, indicating the the numbers of rows of seats. Illustrated is the 11R, available with steel or air suspension and 126 or 150 bhp diesel engine.

1966 Bristol (GB)
VR/NS6G

The Bristol Omnibus Company took delivery of this large 80-seater ECW/Bristol VR double-decker bus in 1966. The bodywork was produced, as on many other Bristol chassis, by Eastern Coach Works of Lowestoft in Suffolk (Body No. EX11). The staircase to the upper deck was located behind the driver's seat. Note the fuel filler below the driver's side window and the clean and straightforward lines of the body design. ECW output from 1948 until 1965 was sold almost exclusively to bus-operating companies within the Tilling Group, an integral part of the British Transport Commission. In 1963 the issued share capital of ECW was transferred from the BTC to the Transport Holding Company, from whom Leyland acquired a 25% holding in 1965.

1966 Ford (GB)
R226

Introduced in 1966, the Ford R226 chassis was powered by a 360 CID 128 bhp diesel engine driving through a five-speed gearbox. The example shown featured a 54-seater body, built by Strachans (Coachbuilders) Ltd and called 'Pacesaver' Mark II. It was supplied to Wolverhampton Corporation Transport Department as their first 36-foot single-decker (the majority of Wolverhampton's buses were 72-seater double-deckers).

1966 Kässbohrer (D)
Setra S7

The Setra S7, produced by the old-established German firm of Karl Kässbohrer Fahrzeugwerke GmbH in Ulm/Donau, was a medium-sized luxury coach for 26 to 30 passengers. It was powered by a Henschel Model 522FVT–K diesel engine mounted at the rear and driving through a five-speed gearbox (an eight-speed gearbox was optional). The power output of this engine was 132 bhp. The vehicle was 7.67 metres long and had a wheelbase of 3.63 metres. There was a transverse luggage compartment, below the floor, with a capacity of 3 cubic metres. The name 'Setra' was derived from *'SElbstTRAgend'* which is German for self-supporting, in this case applying to the unitary chassisless construction of the Kässbohrer buses and coaches.

1966 Leyland (GB)
Olympic Mk X

Designed by Leyland in collaboration with Metropolitan-Cammell-Weymann of the Vickers Group, this was a new chassis-less 41-seater transit coach, featuring special equipment to meet extreme weather conditions in North America. The main structure was of integral design, with underframe members of high-grade-steel channel-section carry- ing the vehicle running units and the engine, which was mounted at the rear and which was easily removable in 'power-pack' form for major overhauls. The overall length, over the bumpers, was 39 ft 11 in, the width was 8 ft 6 in. Note the large windscreen wipers with pantograph arms.

1967 Kässbohrer (D)

Setra SG175UL

Before and during World War II, Kässbohrer had built a variety of trailer buses, both of semi- and full-trailer types. About 1960 the company designed an articulated type (*Gelenkomnibus*), which was further developed throughout the 1960s. An example, operated by the city of Neuss, is illustrated here. It had a total capacity for about 175 passengers, depending on specification. The 210 bhp diesel engine was mounted under the floor of the front unit and drove the centre axle through a six-speed gearbox. With an overall length of over 16.5 metres, the bus weighed about 11 tons.

1968 Bristol (GB)
VRL/LH

This large 60-seater VRL type double-decker coach on a Bristol VRL/LH 222-inch wheelbase chassis was supplied in 1968 to Ribble Motor Services Ltd (Standerwick, Preston, Lancs). The long-distance luxury bodywork was constructed by Eastern Coach Works Ltd of Lowestoft and incorporated a toilet area and 250 cu ft luggage compartment at the rear of the lower deck. A 175 bhp six-cylinder diesel engine drove through a five-speed transmission and the brakes were air-operated. The seating capacity was 42 upstairs and 18 downstairs.

1968 Ford (GB)
R226

The 'Viceroy 37' was introduced in 1968 by the Duple Group for the 1969 model year. It was a 53-passenger luxury coach, available on Bedford VAL70 and Ford R226 chassis, an example of the latter is shown. Compared with the earlier 'Viceroy' there were many changes in styling and specification but the basic steel and timber construction remained. The main framing units were all jig-built for standardization and easy accident repair. The 150 bhp Turbo 360 diesel was one of several power units available in the 1969 range of Ford R Series buses and coaches.

1968 Hino (J)
RE100

Introduced in 1968, the Hino RE100 bus was of chassisless unitary construction with rear-mounted underfloor diesel engine. It had a gross vehicle weight of 12,270 kg and seating capacity for 49 persons. A maximum speed of 53 mph was quoted. The six-cylinder diesel engine had a cubic capacity of 9036 cc (551.4 cu in) and developed its maximum power of 175 DIN-bhp at 2350 rpm. It drove through a five-speed constant-mesh gearbox.

1969 Berliet (F)

'Cruisair 3'

In 1969–70, Automobiles M. Berliet of Vénissieux, Rhone, France, offered the 'Cruisair 3' *Grand Tourisme* coach as their largest model. It had luxury seating accommodation for 40 persons, air suspension ('Airlam'), and a wheelbase of 5.76 metres. The 200 bhp diesel engine had six cylinders in V-formation and drove through a transmission with six forward and two reverse speeds. A smaller version, designated 'Cruisair 2', was offered with 32-seater coachwork.

Turbo Cruiser III
TURBO-CRUISER III
GMC
MICHIGAN
13M·186
GREAT LAKE STATE

1969 Magirus-Deutz (D)

170 S11H

Fifty years after the first Magirus bus, the Klöckner-Humboldt-Deutz Mainz works delivered this 'VÖV'-bus to the *Deutsche Bundespost*. VÖV stands for *Verband öffentlicher Verkehrsbetriebe* (Association of Public Transport Enterprises), an organization which had established standard specifications for city buses. These standards applied to engine power (170 to 190 bhp) and location (rear), windscreens, wheelbase (5.6 metres), overall length (11 metres), turning circle (20.5 metres), floor height (0.71 metre), suspension (air), brakes (dual circuit), seats, paintwork and etc. KHD introduced their first 'VÖV'-bus in 1967, the 170 S11N, to be followed by variants like the 170 S11H and M, the latter being a mid-engined model for Cologne.

1969 GMC (USA)

Turbo-Cruiser III

This impressive transit bus was an experimental vehicle driven by a gas-turbine power unit. It was unveiled in December 1969 by the GMC Truck & Coach Division of the General Motors Corporation. At its launching in Washington D.C. and New York City, it was described as 'a potential solution to bus emission problems'. Note the hefty front bumper, towing eyes and typical American styling. GMC is one of America's largest producers of buses and coaches.

1969 Peugeot (F)
J7

The Peugeot J7, basically a panel van, was offered as a 14-seater mini-bus or mini-coach and also as a schoolbus with 28 smaller seats and as a personnel/load carrier with 12 seats. Each version was available with a Model XC5P petrol engine (four-cylinder, 1618 cc, 68 bhp) or a Model XDP90 diesel (four-cylinder, 2112 cc, 75 bhp). The latter was designated J7D. Both had a four-speed gearbox in which third and top gear were under- and overdrive respectively. Drive was to the independently-sprung front wheels.

1970 Bedford (GB)
YRQ

Vauxhall Motors introduced a new passenger chassis with mid-mounted vertical six-cylinder diesel engine in 1970. It had a 193-inch wheelbase, air-assisted hydraulic brakes and 8.25–20 tyres. The engine developed 146 bhp and drove through a five-speed gearbox. The mid-chassis location of the engine was claimed to ensure quiet and comfortable travel. It was developed from the well-known VAM chassis of the 1960s, which it superseded. Example shown is a 'Viceroy' luxury coach by Duple Coachbuilders Ltd. This coachwork was also fitted on Ford R1114 and other chassis.

1970 Bristol (GB)
RELH6G

One of several types of coaches mounted on this Gardner-engined 222-inch wheelbase chassis was this 45-seater by Eastern Coach Works (Body No. 18156). It was delivered in 1970 to the Western National Omnibus Company Ltd (Royal Blue) whose headquarters are in Exeter. The Gardner six-cylinder diesel engine was coupled to a five-speed transmission, brakes were air-operated and the GVW was 25,360 lbs; 47-seaters were also available.

1970 Daimler (GB)

'Fleetline'

Doncaster Corporation in Yorkshire are the operators of this Daimler 'Fleetline' double-decker. The bodywork was built by Charles H. Roe Ltd of Cross Gates Carriage Works, Leeds. Roe produced the same bodies also on the Leyland 'Atlantean', a similar rear-engined chassis. The bus features a forward entrance, centre exit layout and was designed for one-man operation. The 'Fleetline' can also be supplied for single-decker bodywork and there is a choice between a Leyland or Gardner engine. Daimler Transport Vehicles of Coventry is now a member of British Leyland's Truck & Bus Division.

1970 Mercedes-Benz (D)
O302

By 1969–70 the Mannheim plant of Daimler-Benz AG offered 20 variants in the O302 range, namely touring coaches with high side windows (O302 Üh, 10–13 seat rows), inter-city buses with high or low side windows (O302 Ünh and Ün, 10–13 seat rows), city buses with high or low side windows (O302 Sth and St, 10–12 seat rows), and a city bus with extra wide four-leaf entrance door in front of the front axle and high side windows (O302 SthD, 11 or 12 seat rows). Models with 10 and 11 seat rows had a 130 bhp engine, the others had a 170 bhp engine. A special stainless-steel bodied O302 Üh is shown.

1970 Volvo/Van Hool (S/B)
B58–55T

The well-known bus and coach manu-facturing firm, Van Hool & Sons of Koningshooikt in Belgium, produce body-work on a variety of bus chassis but specialize in their own designs which are integral buses and coaches entirely of their own manufacture with the exception of engine and running gear. For a long time Van Hool has used Fiat components almost exclusively (Van Hool–Fiat) but suitably modified, the same basic body-work can be mounted on chassis made by Volvo (shown), Leyland, Bedford, DAF, Daimler-Benz, etc. In addition to coaches ranging from small 18-seaters up to 55-seaters and city buses, the company (which is run by the founder Bernard van Hool and his eight sons) produce semi-trailers of many types.

1971 AM General (USA)

Flyer

In 1971 it was announced by the American Motors Corporation that this 53-passenger diesel transit bus would be produced in Mishawaka, Indiana, by its subsidiary AM General Corporation. AM General obtained worldwide rights to manufacture and market Flyer buses, following an agreement with Flyer Industries Limited of Winnipeg, Canada and they also became the only US producer of electric transit buses.

1971 Citroën (F)

T55

The Citroën T55 passenger chassis with 5.33-metre wheelbase was first introduced in 1957 and remained in production for many years. Of conventional design, it was offered with various types of power units, namely the Type 94×110 (4.58-litre) petrol engine, the Type 100×110 (5.18-litre) petrol engine and the Type 100 (5.18-litre) diesel. All had six cylinders with overhead valves and 110-mm piston stroke. Cylinder bore was 94, 100 and 100 mm respectively. A city bus with coachwork by Heuliez is shown.

1971 Ford (GB)

'Transit'

One of a large range of bodystyles in the Anglo–German Ford Transit range: the British-built Transit 130 long-wheelbase 17-seater Crewbus. This model has a 118-inch wheelbase and dual rear tyres. The standard power unit is a 2.0-litre (1996 cc), four-cylinder petrol engine developing 85.5 bhp (93 bhp for high-compression variant) with a Ford 2.4-litre (2360 cc) diesel as optional equipment. The diesel has an output of 54 or 61 bhp (low or high rating). 'Transit' Crewbuses have longitudinal seats in the rear.

1971 Hino (J)
RE100 P

An underfloor rear-engined 4.8-metre wheelbase coach of frameless integral construction with seating capacity for up to 51 passengers (shown as special purpose model with separated rear compartment). It is equipped with exhaust brake, a choice of five-speed constant-mesh manual gearbox or automatic transmission and is powered by a six-cylinder-9-litre diesel of 175 bhp, giving maximum road speed of 57 mph. The overall dimensions are 10.00×2.46 metres, the kerb weight is 7600 kg, and the GVW is 14,000 kg. Optional equipment includes air suspension and power steering. Produced 1968–72.

1972 Ford (GB)
'Transit'

In Maidstone, Kent, a new idea in public transport was launched in 1972. Called Dial-A-Ride, it provides local residents with their first door-to-door bus service at moderate cost. Pioneered by Ford of England, the taxi-like system was soon under close scrutiny by many local authorities and private transport operators all over Britain. Here, one of the Strachans-bodied 16-seater Ford 'Transit' buses is seen swinging into action at the beginning of its daily programme.

1972 Nissan (J)
PR105

One of a variety of forward control buses offered by the Nissan Diesel Motor Co. Ltd of Japan, it provides accommodation for 49 persons and can travel at a maximum speed of 65 mph. The engine is a water-cooled six-cylinder diesel, mounted at the rear and developing its maximum power of 190 bhp (SAE) at 2300 rpm. The piston displacement, or cubic capacity, of the engine is 10,308 cc (629 cu in). Curb weight and GVW are 8280 kg (18,254 lbs) and 11,085 kg (24,438 lbs) respectively, the wheelbase is 5.25 metres (206.7 in). Brakes are of the dual-circuit air-actuated type, the top gear of the five-speed constant-mesh gearbox is an 0.789:1 overdrive.

1972 Saurer (CH)
5DUK–A

A large-capacity bus with Saurer air suspension and underfloor engine, which is also available under the Berna name, as Berna 5VUK–A. It has a carrying capacity of 27 seated passengers and 75 standing, with one two-leaf entrance door and two exits. It is also available with a single exit and different seating layout, offering accommodation for 50 seated and 24 standing passengers (Saurer 5DUK, Berna 5VUK). The engine is a 215 bhp 12-litre six-cylinder diesel, driving through a Diwabus automatic transmission (Model 5DUK/5VUK has epicyclic transmission with four forward speeds plus overdrive). The wheelbase is 5.80 metres, overall length and width is 11.70 by 2.50 metres (Model 5DUK/ 5VUK is slightly smaller and has a 5.50-metre wheelbase). Air brakes with dual circuits are fitted.

1973 Ford (GB)
R1114

The 'Panorama Elite III' is a modern coach with straight clean lines, large window glass area and luxury seating for 53 passengers. It is produced by Plaxtons of Scarborough, on AEC, Bedford, Daimler, Ford, Leyland, Volvo and other chassis and the specimen shown is on the Ford R-Series chassis, which has a 6-litre Turbo diesel engine of 141 bhp (DIN). The gearbox is six-speed with five-speed semi-automatic optional. This coach was first introduced at the International Commercial Motor Show in Earls Court, London, in September 1972; the curved side windows are a noteworthy feature. Plaxtons also produce a slightly different version with wider doorway and other modifications, called the 'Elite Express III'.

1973 Checker (USA)
'Aerobus Limousine'

This unusual photograph shows an eight-door 12-passenger 'Aerobus Limousine' produced by Checker Motors Corporation of Kalamazoo, Michigan and intended for applications where a station wagon is too small and a bus too large and costly. In the USA, several firms have converted standard passenger cars, e.g. the front-wheel drive Oldsmobile 'Toronado', into 12-seater buses but the Checker model is purpose-built. The wheelbase is 189 inches and the overall length is $270\frac{3}{4}$ inches. The 1973 model is powered by a 5.7-litre Chevrolet V8 engine and has full power for steering and brakes. Automatic transmission is standard equipment.

Index